To Embroider the Ground with Prayer

MADE IN MICHIGAN WRITERS SERIES

General Editors
Michael Delp, Interlochen Center for the Arts
M. L. Liebler, Wayne State University

Advisory Editors
Melba Joyce Boyd
Wayne State University

Stuart Dybek
Western Michigan University

Kathleen Glynn

Jerry Herron
Wayne State University

Laura Kasischke
University of Michigan

Frank Rashid
Marygrove College

Doug Stanton
Author of *In Harm's Way*

A complete listing of the books in this series
can be found online at wsupress.wayne.edu

To Embroider the Ground with Prayer

Poems by Teresa J. Scollon

Wayne State University Press

Detroit

© 2012 by Wayne State University Press, Detroit, Michigan 48201.

All rights reserved. No part of this book may be reproduced without formal permission.

Manufactured in the United States of America.

16 15 14 13 12   5 4 3 2 1

Library of Congress Cataloging-in-Publication Data

Scollon, Teresa J., 1962–

To embroider the ground with prayer : poems / by Teresa J. Scollon.

p. cm. — (Made in Michigan writers series)

ISBN 978-0-8143-3620-5 (pbk. : alk. paper) — ISBN 978-0-8143-3621-2 (ebook)

I. Title.

PS3619.C634T62 2012

811'.6—dc22

2011028209

∞

Designed and typeset by Maya Rhodes

Composed in Berkeley and Cronos Pro

In memory of my father, who loved stories.

Contents

I am grateful to my family and community for the relationships and experiences that have inspired and supported me. I should say that while real events and people were sources of inspiration, these poems are works of imagination and memory—that most flawed, individual, and treasured filter—and may not be read as factual works. Real people and events have been teased apart, conflated, recombined, and changed to serve the needs of the poems. Some things are entirely made up. I hope these poems will create a world of their own, in which the details may or may not be factual, but in which the sentiments are true, and deeply felt.

I am grateful to Interlochen Arts Academy for its support of this manuscript through the Writer-in-Residence program.

I also thank the National Endowment for the Arts for its support while this manuscript was completed.

Thank you to the editors of the journals in which some of these poems first appeared. These journals include the *Atlanta Review*, *Damselfly Press*, *Dunes Review*, *Nimrod*, *Off Channel: 2009 Anthology*, *Spoon River Poetry Review*, *Third Coast*, and *Wisconsin People and Ideas*.

Several poems appeared in the chapbook *Friday Nights the Whole Town Goes to the Basketball Game*, published in 2009 by the Michigan Writers Cooperative Press.

I am deeply grateful to all who assisted in midwiving these poems. My family, friends, teachers, and village have all held me close. I hold them close in return.

To Embroider the Ground with Prayer

The Invitation

When I woke, I was already in her arms.
She was carrying me down the hall to the night
and the glimmering crickets. I knew her.

I had a name and she was speaking it.
I knew my name and she was telling me
it was all right, saying come out

and see the stars the beautiful stars
with her and Daddy and little John. Then
we were out in the soft night, on the front step

with the crickets and wet grass all around.
She showed me the stars; I heard their voices.
I sat wrapped in a pink blanket while Johnny danced

on the lawn, held up his arms to my father,
who swung him around on the grass under the stars.
I was waking, waking into something

already in motion, like the soft shaking
of an earthquake, rolling me side to side.
That night they were young, passing

into my arms the possibility of stars,
a sheer vase for the capture of flowers,
the thin and meltable film of memory.

Later there would be other stars. Later
I would rise up; I would run down
that hall to see her upright, raging

against the newest children in the house,
who sat frozen and wrapped in their beds,
their faces the brightness of hammered glass.

Later the house would be full of voices as angry
as separate oceans. They would spill out.
I would spill out. I would rise up

and hand back to them their rage, the broken
vase of memory. But the stars still and always
live there. When I left that house

I carried my name. The way ginger
lights the inside of my mouth,
I carry that night. Johnny still holds

up his arms. Like waves we all return,
are thrown every year back to the step
for a photograph. Together we paste

a thin film of happiness over the waves
of ground formed by heavings and erosions,
planted over with living things.

That night's invitation brings me
to the thin moment of a poem, to each word
placed for its brightness. I carry her with me

and when I look at the sky, she looks with me.
When I woke, we were already moving
toward the night, toward the crickets and the stars.

We were both waking, she and I.
She was calling the name she had given me.
I was already in her arms.

Drought Year

He was sick in a drought year: a time when ruin comes
　　in increments—each sunrise,
each cloudless noon brings a thousand tiny deaths
　　and panic lies clock-heavy
on the chest, counting, counting—

One morning, he told me, he couldn't sleep
　　so he got up and drove out
to look at the parched fields, the screen door's
　　creak the only sound
in the quiet house. Where he lived, the fields lie flat
　　and open, ancient lake bed

young to this air—the only place his fear
　　could spread and quiet.
He passed rows and rows of midsummer's growth:
　　white beans and corn.
Faster and faster, a sea, a blurred sea of green
　　and sage green, then slower,

rows and rows again. He knew the rows were
　　a farmer's spring prayer
put into the ground pass by pass: the steady knocking
　　journey down the rows,
the tractor's heat and drum, the tense muscle-focus
　　as the row end approaches,

hard left steer into a teardrop turn, definite pull
to raise the planter,
then hard right, and at this moment, everything
is tight and engaged—
the animal tractor spinning, dirt spit out
under its wheels,

the wide sweep of the raised planter, a feathered fan
swinging behind,
like the wheel and stomp of the Sandhill, courting.
The weighted sway
of the planter, movement in an old circle, heading
by feel toward what lies ahead—

this is the farmer's dance for each row's end, each row's
beginning, new hope
ribboning behind. Now at midsummer, each young
plant was hunched against
further loss, its leaves shuttered and luminous,
the pale undersides

thrown up and glimmering. *Not enough. What if
there is not enough?*
Rain. Life. Time. This is the world my father knew:
the farmer's returning
again and again to embroider the ground with prayer,
the rows of small lives, great birds

calling overhead, the girlish twirl of the earth around
    the sun, all balanced
in a great delicate blackness larger than our knowing,
    larger than our imagined
God. But this morning it began to rain, a whisper,
    so soft it had to be noticed,

and he saw the crops as they stood under the rain.
    The shuttered leaves began
to open in the slow, wondrous way plants move.
    They reached up for more
in the loved gesture of trees, that motion of hope,
    to take in whatever comes.

He told me when it began to rain, he saw the crops
    saying *thank you, thank you, thank you.*
He was trying to tell me this is all beautiful, this is all
    so beautiful. He drove
a little longer, slowing, his arm propped in the open
    window, feeling

rain bead on his arm, *that loved arm*, moisture
    beading on his face.
And moving slowly, he let himself be turned,
    gently, toward home.

Mid-Life, I'm Lost

Traveling like this, I envy the forest
its full cellar of roots. Hurrying

like this, I envy the dawdling rain,
and snow, how it chooses to arrive

only in the right conditions. I envy leaves—
they have such simple relocations—

and isn't a tree a seed's commitment
to its place on the ground, its one

true shape? I'm caught the way water
stands in spring, outside its normal

channels, forced to pool or run
when there's no place to settle.

I hear full rivers underground,
but I'm as dry as a winged seed,

too light to sink or take root.
I cannot rest. I'm an envious wind

rattling the branches of other lives.

Reciprocity

Horse Piss Wilson is out
working in the yard.
His wife leans out
the kitchen window.

"H.P.," she says, "you better
get in here and get cleaned up,"
she says. "Aren't you going
to the neighbor's funeral?"

"Hell, no," he says. "He ain't
going to mine."

Autobiography: Falling

How a bird falls
from a height
from a great height
says something about
confidence.

The bird lets itself drop
and its dropping
is curiously
slow.

The word plummet
has a place where
for a moment
the mouth holds
a plum.
For only a moment.
The roundness
of it is how
a bird falls.

There is weight
and also the use of weight
before catching
the final updraft.
The one so low
it tousles
the heads
of the grass.

Seven loves and I never
fell. My mouth could not
form that O.

Except once I fell. Once
I did fall. O it was a long
way down.
There was no
updraft.

My mother told me
she didn't love
my father
when they married
but she saw
he was a good man.

Once she knocked over
a table in anger
and when he bent
to right it,
she pushed him.
I was afraid
he would fall.

Last week
I fell on the street.
The ground came up
and I unfolded.
My hands slid as far
as they could.
Then my ribs
and my belly
hit the ground.

I cried out
from the back of my throat,
from the center of me,
the way birds do.
The O was in my mouth.
My mouth would not close.

He picked me up so easily
and set me on my feet.
This was the man
who fell for me but I
couldn't, I
wouldn't.

After I fell,
while I recovered
I sat on the porch
and noticed the birds.

If I could fly
maybe my bones
would lighten.
Maybe I could see

everything. Maybe love
would not look
like a trench
circling the earth.

Family Music

Banging on holidays like a piano tuner—
this tone, tone, tone, then the octave, then
the triad, then another note—we work
around the calendar of keys, muscling
swollen pegs and frayed wires into tune.

We forget how all this internal weather,
this spitting turbulence, warps the fine grain
of wood, how wood is a living material,
breathing and absorbing even after it's cut
and fashioned into a living room shape.

If we chopped it up and lit a fire, we'd hear
water hiss and wail as it heats and escapes
each cellulose room—each ring another year
of growing in concentric direction—all of it
finally released. That would be music.

The Yoga Master at the Party

said to me,

    I wouldn't worry about your hands

    because your heart is opening

and I thought

    how smugly he shared

    this self-satisfied horseshit

and at the same time

    I felt the rose blooming

    in my chest

and if even this guy

    could feel it

    it must be true.

Omniscient or oblivious,

    he shifted his attention

    to the dancer beside me.

I saw how he shaped

    his spew to spell:

    Please, appreciate me.

The dancer was kind.

    He swallowed hard and looked at the ceiling

    as if he was trying to understand.

The yoga master introduced

    two more healers: the massage student

    and the pranic healer with her divining rod.

    They needed love too.

The circle expanded.

> The massage student went after the labor activist
> at his request: his hands were hurting.

While she worked, the labor activist

> looked gently into the massage student's face
> and asked her questions.

Meanwhile, her husband went on

> about his sciatica. *She has*
> *healing hands*, he said.

Divining rods everywhere

> quivered in anticipation
> of the next tender need.

Later, the yoga master left,

> still lonely but a bit emptier.
> I left too, no fuller than any mirror,

but still, I have my heart

> and
> it's opening.

Catechism

On the way out to the barn Dad mentioned old Father Fedewa—
how he put the fear of God into them, insisted they were all
going to Hell. "That kind of marks you for life," he said.

I listened to the road and the wet slush running underneath
the truck. "You believe in Hell?" I asked. "No," he said.
We let the road run for a moment. I asked, "You believe

in Heaven?" The road took its turn. "About as much
as I believe in Hell," he said. Now we had a rhythm
going—we were talking like real cowboys, tough talk

about God with no helping verbs or sissy lead-ins—
a few words against the hard wind of the road and getting a kick
out of it. Here was my chance to quiz the man

responsible for my religious upbringing. I looked
for a high-stakes question: "You believe Christ rose
from the dead?" He gave this the moment of thought

it deserved, tooling along in his truck. Finally, he said,
"Well, I'm all right until I get to the boulder."
And we were tickled. He might be God, He might be

the Son of God, He might even be the Risen God,
but that boulder was just too much. We rolled
for a little, feeling how delight rises from somewhere

and is held in the throat. Then I asked, "You believe
Communion is the body and blood of Christ?" He got
quiet. The question hung there in the cab. Maybe

I'd gone too far. He said, in a low voice, "No."
Maybe he'd gone too far. I asked him, quietly,
"So what are you thinking when you're handing out

the Host on Sundays to all the people?" and I felt
dangerous, but I wanted to know how he'd explain.
In that pause he might have had a million answers,

whole histories—enough to found a people on.
But there was joy here, and an opportunity for devil-
ment. In his most sly and solemn tone he said,

"You dummy." We both knew we could say
the same thing about him. We chuckled and shifted
and shook our heads, watched the snow fall

on the windshield, and wondered. Let mystery
be mystery; let all the explanations be ridiculous;
let us be together in the distance between.

July Fourth

One year ago today you rode in the village parade
at the invitation of the friend who sat beside you:
a stiff-legged farmer dressed as the Easter Bunny—
his costume as randomly strange

as everything else that was happening to you.
I watched you from the curb. You were waving
and waving, grinning, your face still rosy,
your scalp balding under the campaign hat.

You'd retired from office before you got sick
but he'd asked you to dress as Mr. America,
so you dug out your campaign posters,
bright red with bone-white letters.

We'd agreed it'd be good for the town to see
you. Stories had you half buried already,
and we were all so broken, panicked
but not saying so. And you relished the joke

of a sick man running for office, so Irish
in its blackness—nothing funnier than disaster.
And it *was* funny, you in the street before us, smiling,
leaning out of the little rig as if about to spring

into conversation with us. How you loved to laugh
and greet people—that ritual and talent of mammals:

greeting—and you were so good at it, rolling in
with a grin and a little crack, laughing

at yourself and this comic predicament,
this terror, we share. And we loved you
for it. People still talk about your smile.
Here in our town on July Fourth, it was good

for us to see you. It was good for you to hear us
calling to you. It was good for all of us
to smile and wave and heal each other
for that mile and a half of public sun.

Friday Nights the Whole Town
Goes to the Basketball Game

Nick said, "Listen, Bill,
this is no joke. Chinese
tanks. Chi. Nese. Tanks,

Bill. Were spotted rolling up
I-75. What you think you know
about the United Nations

is *lies, lies,* spread
by an international conspiracy
to take over our homeland.

We've got to protect our country,
protect our constitutional right
to bear arms. But I'm ready.

I'm ready. I've got guns
and ammunition
buried in my front yard.

I'm warning you—
you'll regret it
if you don't do the same."

Bill said, "Nick,
Nick, whaddya thinking?
What if the Chinese

show up in February,
Nick? This is Michigan,
for chrissake. How're you

going to get those guns
out of your front yard
when the ground is frozen?

Whaddya gonna do then,
Nick?"

John's a Teacher

I tell people
I repeat myself
for a living,

and nine times out of ten
the guy I'm talking to
says,

"—What?"

Doc Tells a Story on Horse Piss Wilson

Old Horse Piss bought a stud
named Royal Eye Frisco.
And Royal Eye Frisco had killed
a man, everybody knew
it, he was
wild.

So H.P. called me to come out one day
and treat the bugger.
He'd been breeding him
and his penis got bent,
so it was all swollen up.
I had to give him a shot
of cortisone.

Well, I went out there with my bag
and I must have been shaking,
my hands must have just
been a-shaking
while I got the shot ready.
And old Royal Eye Frisco was tied up,
and he's stamping,
and he's pawing,
and he's rolling
his eyes. He was
wild.

Well, old Horse Piss must have seen me shaking.
He grabbed a BB gun he had
standing in the corner there

and he just sprayed
old Royal Eye Frisco from side to side,
blammity-bam-bam!

That old horse just stopped and stood there,
and his legs were just as stiff,
and his eyes were just as wide,
he was just
a-quivering.

And old Horse Piss looked at me and said,
"*Now* you can treat the sonofabitch."

Goodbye to Dwight Lipke

The day before Thanksgiving is the day
Dwight Lipke came to say goodbye
to my father. Dwight's moving to the Florida Keys.

He's got a trailer there and, he says, a girlfriend.
He never dated here, but now it's all new.
The store is closed, his parents dead and buried,

even the little house he lived in all his fifty years
is sold—it took awhile, on account of the strong
smell of cat piss. He must have loved

those cats to count the vet among his friends.
Dad says, "Dwight was near tears, I think;
I kind of had to cut him off a little bit,"

and I realize Dad had hurried in order to talk
to *me*. I say, "That's all right, there was no rush."
And I wish I was there to call out to the back

of departing Lipke, *Hey, come back, say your goodbye.*
He'll miss you. I'm on the phone with my dad
to tell him I can't make it home for Thanksgiving.

He would never say *please come*, and because of this
I don't know if he ever feels *please come*.
We get to talking about jokes, about what is funny

in a joke, how there's a little twist, a little laugh,
but then you turn a corner and the real thing
knocks you down; you gasp or laugh

involuntarily—your body knows before your mind
does. Lipke is like that. Why do I think it's sadder
to leave home at fifty than at sixteen?

It strikes me that way. Or the way Dad asked
very fast, "So are you coming up?" He's standing
in his clinic, calling me, saying goodbye

to Dwight Lipke, all kinds of wishes let loose
in the room, knocking up against glass doors
and animal print wallpaper, clinging

near the ceiling. But it's no use. Lipke
is gone and he's not ever coming back.
I'm too far away. After we hang up,

I'm still listening. I know my father
will quietly close the door, and go
into the house for another cup of coffee.

Death and the Photocopier

My father is on the other side of the river
now. I'm here with his ashes, fluttering
scraps of paper in my hands, an immigrant

among people who never knew him.
I've only a clutch of articles to show
he lived, he died—pages of the book

I'm torn from—I'm standing over
the machine in a corner of the office
making copies: light and hum, memory,

the fragile drum, bright hot attention
to each detail, the same hard pull and pause
of the rhythm of oars, of hard sobbing.

This is so contained. What I want is to lie
down full length with my hair spread over
a grave, weeping. I want to be still

floating between life and death, on the river
with its fine filtered mist and its view of both banks,
his body still warm, his breath

lingering over our heads. But he's left
his cooled ashes behind, and he's already
trekking deep into the country beyond the bank.

I can't see him anymore. I'm left here
on the stranger shore, trying to explain my passage.
Making copies under false light, in a place

where paper is seen as merely paper,
and not as the remains of living trees,
not as the breath before ashes.

Exile

This is exile: long car trips punctuated by stops to find
a newspaper or walk an animal, searching for a bearable
song on the radio, jotting down lines of poetry on gas receipts—

journeys threaded by the review of my history: how I left,
how I again left, all those hollow years. I drive back
and forth to continuously reestablish: this is my life,

this was my life, this is the distance between these two
lives. I feel this geography in my bones. Four states away,
Melanie, I know you are weaving the same journey.

Meanwhile, our befuddled fathers are wandering their towers,
dying. Our fickle kings, who refused to travel
or speak in our defense, who saw us to our boats

when home was closed to us. How we loved them!
And don't you wonder: did they ever pace the beach,
watching for our ships? I watch other ways of living:

new spiders emerge with ready parachutes and no memory
but what DNA provides. *Jump!* And they do.
Me, I am always looking over my shoulder, back

at the shore I left, forced into an old calling:
truth-teller, itinerant, wanderer, ever making story
to weave some kind of bed.

You and I, we did make homes: islands of quiet,
plush with healers, with patient animals who lie down
with us to sleep. Flowers, wine, and altars

to peace and forgiveness, to fill the empty gourds
of ourselves. God is so evident on our islands—
a naked cliff on the ocean side, or the bony ledges

of reflection. It's not easy to lie down on this God,
to get comfortable. It's not easy to look at our histories
and not wish for sixty years spent in one fertile valley.

Ah, but this is wishful thinking. There would still be stones
in that valley. God is what's left after years of drought
and poor farming: all the topsoil blown away.

Grief in the Morning

rises, like dough warmed in the oven

all night and filling the air
with the aroma of small live things.
Huge as a swollen waterskin,

it needs attention: to be punched
down to a manageable size,
crammed back into the oven

before it again rises. I'm getting
a late start, resolve to leave
sorrow in the shower with the weeping

tile, but grief follows me out
of the house. This is my dowry,
my jeweled pack animal,

its broad and decorated feet
plodding behind me. We sway
and pick along a path.

I swish scarves. The ground
quivers with little bells.
At night I'll lie down again

with grief, this knobby bedfellow—
all elbows and crowding the middle,
and so heavy, all night the bed

is a ditch I roll into.

Conference Room in Bloomington, Minnesota

"Effective Problem Solving is just what we need
around here," says the guy who keeps everybody pepped up,
his guts pushed up into the hearty voice

of a sportscaster. The rest of them when questioned
say where do you start, ha-ha, but one does have
a problem now that he thinks about it: the deer he shot

last weekend in North Dakota and no place to keep it
cold, the normal method (several deer hanging
by their throats in a semitrailer) being kaput on account

of the unseasonable warm weather. Which is a real
problem. Which points to the larger problem of global warming,
but no one here is willing to take that on. Let's keep it

in the room, keep it to something we can handle. We're
more focused on how long our laptop batteries will go
before recharging or the new place we find ourselves in,

between a rock and a hard policy, having to explain things
we never got a chance to write. And the dealers don't like it,
and who can blame them? They're used to the old way

and it's a very emotional topic for them, but expectations
have to change and we have to lay it out for them, just lay it out,
that's all there is to it, and hey, maybe we're the ones

who have to adjust. Talking to management is like praying
or the proverbial message in the bottle—you never know
if it's getting through, never can be sure, but it must have

worked at least once, otherwise we wouldn't all know about it.
Also, some problems are more easily solved than others.
The copy problem, for example. We just asked Marlene

and gave her five bucks since she's just back from two weeks
vacation and not too happy about it so we'd better make sure
we get the projector back to her by four. The other materials

never did arrive, but you learn to improvise, that's what you do.
We're used to it, and anyway we ditched the agenda by noon—
it was too basic, a waste of these people's time and the video

outdated, but once it probably seemed like a great thing,
that's where we were then, but now we're in the here and now.
After it was all over we went downstairs to the bar. They took

me along for a beer to talk things over, or more accurately, to keep
each other company in the middle of these problems. Some talked more,
some thought more and smoked while they did so. Works for me.

The Old Horse

The Ten Commandments were posted on the porch.
Inside, women wrapped in skirts and head cloths.
Dad and I stepped in from another tribe
in our overalls, and waited for the man of the house

to pull on his boots. It was cold, so cold Dad cursed
the weather. The horse was lying on its side
on the cold ground in the barn. It'd been given to the kids,
since it was gentle and old. Dad peeled back

its upper lip to show us how old race horses
were marked with tattoos. We all pushed and pulled
and rolled that horse up onto its belly and then
onto its feet, but it quickly lay down again.

There was no moving it. Dad said, "Well, keep it
warm as you can, use blankets and straw,
and see if it makes it through the night."
He ran some glucose into it, got empty milk jugs

from the truck to use for hot water bottles.
Again he cursed the cold and the sharp wind.
On the way home he asked me, "What kind of a religion
was that in that house?" I asked, "Is that horse

going to make it?" He said, "You never know.
That horse was closer to death than they knew,
lying down like that. You can't keep it warm enough.
And this weather." He told me how he once saved old Duke's colt.

Duke had seven sons and a temper and a colt
that nobody thought would make it. But Duke took a liking
to the young vet and called him out. Dad told him about all
he could do was keep it warm. Duke stayed up all night

to keep that colt in hot water bottles and it made it.
"And after that," Dad said, "I was golden in his eyes.
But you never know. That colt could just as well have died.
It's all chance, what lives and what dies."

This was the time he and I went out to see an old horse
in a cold barn, dying far away from its history.
This was before he knew he was sick. Before we knew
he was already marked. He just couldn't keep warm.

Pigeon Lady

The one on my street
has stepped out of all
the pantheons, disguised

in faded jackets and knitted
caps. She appears daily
to look after these small ones.

If I walk too close
she stops, stands motionless
as a tree, or a god. The people

from Lincoln Park push
past her, past the birds,
in search of hip vintage

and cheaper rent. See their
heels and fitted coats,
their manufactured hair.

How visible they are, how blind,
missing the tousled one
who keeps this street awash

in flutter. She pauses,
opens her bag. It's a quiet
mind that gathers grain,

that remembers the hunger
of unloved birds. The soft nut
of her face bends toward

beauty: see the pigeons,
mottled and barred, as infinitely
variable as snowflakes, strutting

and bowing on lavender feet,
circling her with a skirt
of feathers. She moves, the skirt

flames and scatters, and the air
is suddenly nerved
with a hundred small wings.

for Melanie, Kristen, and Kathleen

New Year's Day, Winslow Beach, Maine

As if the sun opened the sky for us,
as if we could make a new life rise
out of our collision with the sea,

as if the first day's courage could carry us
forward, frightened and alive, we opened
our clothes, ran naked into the ocean's

bottomless cold. We howled, scattered
our fears for the ocean to swallow.
Such soft small animals we are!—

who feel the pull of tides and moon,
the chill of winter water, our shawl of sun.
How beautiful each body is, how light

the notes of our voices, each of us
a small warm sea, standing in the endless
ocean. The delicate cups of our hands

brought water to our faces; the ocean
held a floor of sand under us, waited
for us to tip back onto the beach, cleansed

with water and salt, gasping. What had
we been afraid of? We laughed,
our skin exclaiming, our eyes new stars.

A Meeting with the Game Wardens

I knew I was in when they invited me up
after dinner to unwind. Eight armed men,
each twice my size, in a hotel room—
exactly the kind of situation mothers warn

their daughters to avoid, but I sat down
on the footstool next to Burcz. We were all
exhausted. The Chief let himself sink
onto one of the beds and the rest sat

on the other bed, or in chairs, and Engler
had some whiskey but nobody was drinking much.
They sighed and slipped out of their public role
to be ordinary men together, though they kept

an eye on me the way cops do, seeming relaxed
but alert to every possible direction.
Pretty soon it got hot in there and we
were redfaced. I regretted wearing a skirt

since I had to concentrate on keeping my knees
together, especially on that footstool,
but there was no way I was going to sit
on the bed. At first we tried chitchat

with the TV on but whoever was flipping channels
was always coming up against some titty shot.
It alarmed us all how much female flesh
was on the TV, though nobody said anything

except *see if there's a game on.* We'd look
at the history channel or the news but then
would come a beer commercial and there we were
again. We were all sweating it until Burcz

said, *TV's a real conversation killer* and we shut it off.
Then there was a little lull, during which
Engler offered everybody whiskey. When the jokes
started, I said quietly to Burcz, *should I stay?*

He thought it'd be all right so I smiled
thinly. That was enough to move things along
and pretty soon the Ole and Lena stories began,
which always take place on their wedding night—

all kinds of encounters and confusions. Pretty soon
the master storytellers made themselves known,
Jansen and Burcz, tossing joke after joke
into the room, their Norwegian accents thickening

and Ole and Lena virtually there, rosy and plump,
sitting on the bed. The one about reading the newspaper
during sixty-nine—we feared this joke
would have us all embarrassed with apologies later

and boundaries drawn but Jansen was irresistible,
how he drew Ole and Lena, so comic, so trusting,
with Ole pumping straight in from the field
on the tractor, hollering, *Lena, Lena, it's happening, it's happening!*

and Lena saw him coming and ran out
of the outhouse to meet him at the kitchen door

and up they went the stairs together
and up we all went after and there was something

like tenderness in Jansen's voice and the way
we so willingly followed him into the bedroom
to overhear Ole and Lena talking to each other,
high and mild: *Oh, Lena, whaddya say*

we try something a little different? OK, Ole,
that would be all right, and now in Jansen's hands
the story slipped to the side a little and he pulled us
through it slowly on a silken line, adding details

here, there, building with us hardly knowing it
and we climbed bit by bit with him
until all of a sudden the bottom dropped out
and then God! it was funny, it was so funny

we forgot who we were and just rolled,
shouting for air, choking with the joy of it.
Jansen sat beaming and shaking on the bed
and all he could squeak out of his massive body

was a tinny *hee, hee, hee* and that made us laugh
louder. After a while we were able to wipe our eyes,
sigh and settle down, and agree it was a terrible
joke, just terrible but God it was good. And we rested.

The Chief said that was just what he needed to laugh
like that. He rolled off the bed and patted it
to smooth the bedspread. Then the party broke up
since we were all tired and satisfied and now

a little shy. They decided the Chief
would walk me back and the next day
five of them asked me privately, separately,
if I minded the jokes, if I was okay.

Summer Solstice in Black River Falls

The river built this town, pouring sparks through a narrow space.
The founders laid in place everything they needed, all the necessary

buildings: churches, library, courthouse. Main Street stretches
alongside the hardware store, winds up the hill toward St. Joe's.

This could be any town. I could be anyone, moving through it.
It's a perfect evening. The sky is almost without color, it's so clear;

it finally bleeds blue high up, far away. I drive around
and around, looking. No one is here. The yards are mowed

and empty; the porches hold up their flowers. In the whole town,
I see only one man walking up his driveway, looking back

over his shoulder. West of town the community park
unfolds itself in perfect ball fields, a generous expanse

of grass, bridges, benches, the finest American
landscaping. There are no animals, no kids, no disorder.

A generator provides sound. A decoy lists on the manufactured
pond. Back on Main Street, the stoplight and the bank sign

change on schedule. A sprinkler blesses the funeral home lawn.
Outside Uptown Realty, a recording is triggered by my approach:

asks, *Are you looking for a home loan? Try Community Bank!*
Solstice: I'm at the end of my long days, facing the loss of light,

needing a place where I can know and be known. Instead,
I'm trapped like a shark in my own custom of gathering breath,

resting only by lodging myself in current. I start my car and
drive away, the pistons firing in a pattern with no purpose

but movement. South of the bridge, my last view of the river:
glossy and unmoving, like stricken glass. This is what it's come to.

Little Boat

He swallowed, carefully
working his mouth
and throat all the way

down, let his mouth
drop open to show
the pills still on his

tongue, his eyes blank
and puzzled as a dog's.
Did he not hear me?

I leaned down to look
into his face, said,
"Swallow the pill, Dad.

Swallow the pill."
He made the slightest
of gestures: eyebrows

and shoulders lifted
and held—all the language
he had in that moment.

Swelling or silt
in his brain, the thing
he most feared: a pulling

apart of his thought
from his mind,
mind from his body,

drifting out of my reach,
something unmoored
as gently as a little boat

bending away
from its pier, bobbing
on changeable waters.

How My Mother Loves Flowers

First thing she shows me is her morning glories,
seedlings in Dixie cups, her little blue children.

Long ago she planted bulbs: narcissus and tulip.
She made a warm dark of herself and sprouted

homunculi, five little bulbs. She loved how they sprang
for the light above, but once they emerged

they lingered too low to the ground. This bores her.
There are roses but they are too rich for her blood,

too steeped in red; those sensuous pillows
wrapping their legs around the fence they love.

This frightens her—it's not the kind of communion
she's looking for. She wants to climb over walls

and fences, cover them, hide the nature of them.
It's the ambitious climbers she loves best:

morning glories, clematis, big showy blooms
with their pure arch, vault unencumbered,

straight up to the sun and its frantic heat,
flowers that cry, "Love me, love me, love me!"

that beg, "Shine full on my open face!"
that plead, "Make me believe it's still morning!"

Three A.M.: Prelude

Still childless, still wed, I walk the floor,
to pace and birth a new life for myself.
My muscles, playing their imagined role,
push out this bed that once was life itself.

You sleep, but in the building I can hear
steps heavy, headlong down the silent hall—
someone's up, alone, comes down the stair.
The front door slams, and then no sound at all.

I know the cord that wraps around my heart
still tugs with every turn between us, twinned.
How will we grow when we are pulled apart?
This birth's a death, this elegy a hymn.

Tonight there's no blood yet, there's nothing more
than empty clench, the lurching toward the door.

What Opens

I used to think I ran too soon, busting
out of there the way you did once—leaping
across the knotted lawn on Christmas Eve

into the open door of your buddy's moving car,
the front door of the house rollicking on its hinges,
leaving me to answer all the questions:

> *Where is he? Where'd he go?*
> *Why the hell didn't he*
> *take his coat?*

You always did have a flair—those amazing feet
of yours, Jesus-like, in flight, suspended above the suffering
of the frozen grass. Last time those feet figured

in my memory they were hanging off the end of you,
where you lay on the cold tile floor, overcome
by fumes. My mind bobbed free of my body,

which was moving with celestial speed to *open that door*.
I thought of cartoon rabbits, and when did your feet
become so long and floppy, and how would you be able

to run? I used to dream I left you young and tiny in a park,
or in a tall crowd of strangers, and I had to circle back
to carry you away, to keep you with me always,

but I couldn't, I couldn't stay to find you. I left you
there without defenses. I had to run. And now,
what remains is only a statement of belief:

We all have feet. You have to run for yourself.
Sure, I ran first, but I circled back around the house,
the four-mile square, the state of Michigan, our constellation

of phone lines, farms and snarled thresholds, tethered
for years by my wish to stare something in the face, something
as dissipated and poisonous as exhaust. Caught in my spot

on the porch, where I couldn't be seen from inside the house,
even my dreams were of interiors. I used to watch your track
across the yard, your escape from papered hallways, the moment

one becomes only an outline moving, without the weight
of guts or knotted throat. Maybe I wanted to see
a threatening sky outside that door swinging crazy,

a dog turd directly in your path. But now I see
the joy in it, the hilarity, the way you saw an opening door
with only another door in the way. The truth is

you only drove down a couple of houses to drink a beer,
be ordinary again. A door finally opens in this poem
and I can look at what's above me: soundless stars

the beginning of snow and the promise of longer days,
of something else out there, and I'm running for it.

Untitled

One year after your death, the sky
stays white all day.

The trees are definite and unmoving
in their blackness

and the sky is thick and deaf
as a snow blanket.

Juncos and chickadees are mostly gray
birds, and even the goldfinches have given up

their brilliance for this winter.
Words fall onto my page like empty

shells of sunflower seeds. Seeds fall
from the feeder like words

the birds peck and swallow.
All the day the sky. The sky

over the trees. I wait with the sky.
All day nothing happens.

Birds rearrange themselves
on low branches and you

are as absent as color.

Poem to My Brothers and Sisters

I've been listening for days
to the tape our mother made: interviews
with her children—

a sound snapshot of one day,
one year, five children. Each voice a new note.
The youngest of us, only three,

is carefully forming
each k, f, s, repeating the word wol-f-s, wol-f-s,
to get it right,

his voice a soft little bell.
Today, I sit next to a church, using the Internet
to send a signal to Russia,

hoping to reach him.
We are all tuning to this new and invisible frequency,
elusive lasso, sending

jokes and travel advice. I save
each note and tape, moments captured in stone.
Each stone a miracle

of memory I am mining
for compassion, compassion—the word rings like a bell,
calling me deeper in.

Do you know, we live so drowned
in noise that we cannot hear church bells unless
we are sitting next door.

Once, bells this size
might have called us in from the surrounding hills. Once,
faraway riders might have paused to listen.

In my home, a stone,
a series of related stones, a shell, the watercolor
of a solitary man tending a fire—

these draw me out
to love the earth and all the stuff in it.
Out in the world, in the wide

air, sounds call me in.
I am thinking of bells at the moment of miracle—
water turned into wine,

wine into blood, blood
to tears, tears into peals of laughter like bells—
my dreams run away

with me. In and out.
These are the ways we travel and heal. And blood
is always with me. Do you remember

watching our father's hands
part and separate the living innards of animals?
Seeking, sewing, healing.

He never laid a hand
on us, never examined or extracted our pain.
His refusal pains me still.

We fled in all directions
like a handful of coals flung out from the fire—
    marriages, Japan, the broken schools

    of broken cities, the youngest
in Russia, still running, as if distance could cool the hold
    of our first fiery nest.

    (We began warm and tight
against each other. The air above us glowed.)
    And it's true: Movement brings

    a kind of peace. We found
the world outside, and like stones we skipped
    once, twice, and dropped down

    to sandy beds. And there we lie,
buried and precarious. Still, in my dreams I lose children.
    Cars, keys, and children.

    Standing over the bed
of the youngest—he was seven or eight then, lying there—
    I watched the breeze lift

    the light curtains. It was the middle
of the day. I watched him choking on that day's cruel words.
    His generous tears

spilled out of him and shook
his little chest. I wanted to reach into him. He would not
be held. He gritted his teeth

and tried to force his tears
back in. He was trying to drown his little light. Watching
him was also watching myself

hardening into concrete:
man-made stone. I was both parent and sister, forced
to protect you but the first

to leave. If you were truly mine
I would be guilty of abandonment. I am guilty.
You are truly mine.

Living here, now, my own healing
has begun. But now I have ghost limbs: tingling nerves
where I should be able to find

a brother, a sister, a sign of shared
life, four sources of light cast into myself. I am afraid
of calling you endlessly,

alone on this hilltop,
while you ride out of earshot or lie buried in sand.
I am tuning my voice, polishing

tone, modulating every
harsh k, s, f. I am training to ring with just the right note—
  not too bright, but pure,

  stripped of confusion. The kind of voice
that could succeed in calling you in, to name and listen,
  to make music of the words

  between us. Our tears
will be melted stone. I am waiting for the moment of miracle
  when each seed shakes off silt and ash

  to find its way
toward the light. I am waiting for you to stir and emerge,
  blinded, angry, and whole.

The View from Flight 616

I see how our roads hug the sides of mountains
while skirting the possibilities of the valleys,
the deep plush of frozen grasses.

It is this unbearable scale, how you drive
and drive along, but you are always
looking at the same mountain.

And now over the plains I see
how we parse our prairies with straight lines,
then bend our backs, our minds,

to keep them cleared of snow, as if these flat
constructions were the universe and not
this other, blinding, terrible expanse.

The Moon

The moon showed herself to me this morning,
scraping the sky with her changing blade.
I thought of geese flying, lifting themselves
again and again over the disappointments
of highways, walls and parking lots—the ever-changing world.

I thought of the limits of my view through the windshield.
How people change, and changing, throw us
into different orbits. The fear rising in me
is that love, already waning, will disappear
before I see the moon again.

I need to remember this is only morning.
I don't know what lies ahead.
I want the open heart of one who plants
unfamiliar seeds in a greenhouse
and waits. And lets herself be taught.

I want the supple journey of pitch: not hardening
until it claims something precious—the exquisite
short lives of flies; only then the amber drop,
the captured luster of returning sun,
radiant and recombinant gem.

While I Stood in Obedient Line According to the Dictates of Another Round-Trip Ticket

a crewman sat by the airplane's mouth
leaning over a book called *How to Spot
Doublespeak*. The page swam

with yellow lines, and as I peeked
over his shoulder, he was reading it
again. Wonder how often he'd met

Doublespeak. He had the nape
of a true believer; the sagging shoulders
of one who, deceived over and over,

found out too late people were lying
and by now he was tired, so tired
of finding himself here again,

like a goldfish in a bowl—*swim around,
there's the castle; swim around, there's
the castle*. Maybe he was trying

to be wiser. I don't know. I boarded
the plane with my same old bags,
my original business, headed for

the same place I lived before I left.

Commerce

Karl Barzyk was so gentle
you didn't see how big he was.

One night some kid puts his car
in a ditch, calls Barzyk's for a tow.

Karl come out there, says,
"It'll be twenty dollars to get you out."

Kid says OK. Karl hooks him up, hauls him
out, unhooks him, holds out his hand.

Kid has had a change of heart.
"I'm not paying you twenty bucks for that," he says.

Karl puts one hand on the hood,
shoves the car back into the ditch,

holds out his hand.
"That'll be forty dollars," he says.

"In my hand."

The-First-Bob-Ever Handles a Middle East Situation

Talk about your diversity.
I had this gas station in New York,
in a Jewish neighborhood. I had

a cashier, a Middle Eastern guy
with a turban and a bracelet.
He was good, but I didn't want

the customers getting all upset
about the turban. See, this was
during one of those wars—this

time it was bad. So I told the guy
he couldn't wear the turban
on the job. He said,

I'm very sorry, sir—he was
real polite—*but I cannot take off
my turban. It is my religion.*

I told him, *Wear it
at home, but on the job
you have to take it off.*

He said, *I'm very sorry, sir,
I want to keep my job,
but I cannot uncover my head*

to God. I told him, *Look, pal,*
it's against the uniform policy.
Say what you want, but where

I come from, if the boss
says jump, I say how high?
I don't wanna hear

about religion. These guys,
they don't get it. They think
this is some kind of family.

They'd give half the merchandise
in the store away. Just try
to talk to them about shrink.

They say, *He is my brother,*
he is my uncle. How can I refuse him?
How can you run a business

like that? I say, leave your religion
at home, we got enough problems.
But I had to make it work.

So I gave the guy a compromise—
I told him to wear a blue turban,
to match the uniform. We stitched

a company logo on the front.
Everybody seemed happy.
And the first thing I learned

as a manager—if you fire
everybody, you have to work
all the shifts yourself.

Halloween at Gross's Meat Market

Mrs. Kobernik came in
towing two little costumed kids.

"And who do we have here?"
says Jack. "Are these goblins?"

"No," she says,
"dems Koberniks."

A Visit

Grove Weathers came to the house on a snowy afternoon.
He brought two Mason jars full of soup from Jeanine
and insisted on leaving his boots in the breezeway—

no sense bringing mud into the house. I brought him in
in his socks and we stood over Dad where he lay dreaming
in his recliner, wrapped in a crocheted afghan.

I said, "Dad, Grove is here," and Dad opened his eyes
and smiled and said, "Hi, Grove," or maybe, "Yes." I left them
to visit but came back when I heard silence and found

Grove perched on the couch, his big frame hanging
from his shoulders, his hands clasped. I sat down, uncertain,
but something was called for. I didn't know

if I'd ever talked with Grove before, but I'd known
one of his boys, so I mentioned that. Grove told me
about his heart operation, and I asked for a story

of his pet lioness, now dead, named Susie. How he had
loved her, not least because she'd once nipped
a certain scornful country singer on the rear end

and that lady had required a little bit of medical attention.
Do you know, Grove's daughter-in-law had lunch in Chicago
with someone who had heard of Susie the Lion.

Isn't that something? Isn't it something how a story can travel?
And all the while my father lay in his chair, traveling far
into a story we could not follow, into a blessing beyond telling.

I sat near my father, and listened, and Grove brought
stories of the ones he loved. We sat with our useless
hands useless in our laps, and did what we could do.

In time, Grove went out to sit on the step and put on his boots
and speak to my mother, who was puttering in the breezeway.
I heard him say, "It makes you so damned mad, when you think

about all the worthless bastards out there." And my mother,
who had told me—though she had already and permanently
forgotten she had said this—who had told me she was choosing

not to believe that Dad was dying, looked embarrassed
and said, "Oh, Grove." But Grove was clear,
and he had recovered his voice. And he asked her,

"Well, don't you sometimes feel that way?"
And my mother was unable to reply.

The Last Cat

My father's last effort—he was now too weak to stand—
perched on his stool, fitting together a cat's jaw, trying to repair
bone's brittle lace. My job to hold steady, cupping

that tiny and ferocious face; it kept falling apart in our hands.
The cat was silent, its jaw hanging, strange and split,
exposed—the curved teeth, the rose ribbed vault

of the mouth. We fit wire loops over the eyeteeth,
fit the jagged halves, then pulled the wire taut.
But it slipped, and slipped again.

While we worked, the cat's owner stood by, helpless.
My father asked him, "Did it fall? Did it fall?"
The man shook his head; he hadn't seen the cause.

To see that jaw, the quiet cat, its fierceness stripped away—
Only waiting now, only waiting. I had to stop
to put my spinning head between my knees.

My father's ferocity was always silent, a will that kept
him upright on that stool, that nerved his hands, that swept
exhaustion to the side. What blunt fingers we had,

what slender lines of bone. By now, we knew all healing
is improvised, that he was falling; we could not hold him,
and none of us could save him now. But here he worked,

the healer, pale with effort; he had to fix it. Determined and alone.
The last cat watching with the intelligence of the doomed.
The wire kept slipping, its hold too glancing, too slight.

We did everything we could; it kept falling apart in our hands.

At the Crematory

The man at the crematory
had dark lines deep in his palms
like a farmer's. He showed

me the oven, how a flame
would come down from above
to ignite the chest. I thought

how we point to our chests
to indicate "me." I laid my hand
lightly on the cardboard box

just above my father's chest,
where his life last gathered
and left. Yesterday I'd placed

my hand on his forehead,
to remember the shape in my palm.
The box had the shape of him,

higher at the end with his chest
and head. I couldn't speak
so I nodded and stepped through a door

into a cold lobby. For a few hours
I sat in a hard plastic chair,
waiting. My feet were cold

in a building full of ovens. There were
plastic plants covered in a fine dust,
pictures of sunsets with sad

and helpful inscriptions. Nothing else.
I tried to imagine him on fire:
his white skin, long leg bones, his hands.

Near the end, he would hold up his hand
to look at it, or lay it over his mouth
while he rested. Once he asked me,

"Is that your hand?" He couldn't tell.
He was already leaving his hands.
Once or twice I heard the man

in the room behind me. I heard
the scrape and tang of his metal tools.
And once I smelt hot ash.

I thought how a smell is a very small
molecule that has come loose
and has been carried into your nose.

I didn't like to think of him already
coming apart and flying into my nose,
or mixing with all the other ashes

at the crematory. He was mine.
Suddenly the man came through the door,
spoke to me, handed me a small

cardboard box. At first I thought
the weight of it was what shocked me.
I looked at the man—his beard

was painted on, a dark brown stain
ending in a perfect line across
his jaw, like the painted tree trunks

in Oaxaca. I thought of bark, its dust
and crumble, how paint would hold
it close to the tree forever.

I left, the box anchoring my hands,
left some part of my father released
in the air to settle on the plastic palm.

The Widow Talks about Black Holes

I've been there, holding onto the railing for dear life
at the roller rink, wobbly and afraid, stranded on the far side.
The lights go off and the glitter ball sends stars circling

and the graceful lovers skate arm in arm. I can't remember:
Did anyone ever take me in his arms like that? Once I tried
to let the stars guide me, followed those dancing lights, but I crashed

into the wall. Of all those selfish lovers, no one stopped
to help. I hit my head and remembered my little cousin, Willy,
that summer when his mother brought him out to the farm.

She wasn't right, wasn't well. One night she went crazy, shouting
at Willy—he was a brat anyway—knocking his head against the wall
while he screamed. My brother and I hid in the barn

until our parents came home. That's the problem with the universe:
There's never anyone around to rein it in. Things just happen, *big* things,
stars blowing up and stars being born, whole worlds disappearing

and nobody says a thing. Pieces of planets cut loose
in space. They seem to be floating, but believe me, they're moving
so fast they could hurt you. The black hole is just trying

to hang on, to make the universe stop spinning, to fill the empty place
inside. And who doesn't devour what she loves? Snakes swallow
their young—it's universal. If everyone else would stop

careening around for just one second, they might see
the black hole—holding onto all that danger, needing someone
to come and help sop it all up. I know what that feels like:

I have my fears; I have my emptiness. I could store stars in there.

Everything's in Motion

The basketball spins and curves into my hand,
back out over the uneven concrete. The sun
is setting over the lake. Cars go by the park,

collected in batches by traffic lights, holding
their stars in front of them. Overhead the noisy
jewel of a plane skims across the darkening

sky. When I touch his shirt I feel fabric, sweat,
then muscle. Behind it bone and pure motion, intent,
aim. The fine air lets me pass through it, loves me,

leaves a cool stroke on my arm. I can see
a sailboat resting out on the lake. A child's voice
in the background is saying *I want to talk, I want to talk.*

My hips swing easy; I'm suspended in the air
for a moment between steps. We all learn to walk
in the same way—to take that risk. Even trees

launch their leaves out into a weather they can't
predict. The sweet leather puppy of the basketball
noses into my palm. I push her away;

she comes back. At twilight, out on the water
like that, the wind dies down and there is only
the slap of the boat on deep water. The bugs swarm

and the boats with motors start to go in, and you see
how far away the harbor is. You see your little sail,
upright and still. I've been in that boat before.

Now the crickets spread a layer of song
on the ground. It's time to go in. The sun
will go down and come up again. On the lake,

just after dark, the air will rise, give up a breeze,
enough to carry any boat home to shore.

Mitchell's Story

Then there was the time Mitchell, the school bus driver,
pulled the bus over in Gamble's parking lot there,
down by the light. Pulled it over and went after

one of the kids, one of the Matuzaks. Guess he choked him
a little bit or cuffed him, manhandled him anyway,
and the kid ran out the back of the bus, ran home

and told his folks. We had to call Mitchell before the board
and he denied it, swore up and down he didn't do it,
said he'd even take a lie detector test to prove it.

So Klein loaded him up, drove him over to the county
sheriff's to take the test and it showed he was lying. So then
the story all came out. Klein drove him home again

the fifteen miles and Mitchell sat there in the car.
Probably had a minute to think; he looked at Klein and said
"Those lie detectors, they're pretty good!"

So here's Mitchell sitting in the car, being driven
by the superintendent of schools, by a man in a suit jacket.
Being carried for once. Wrong, proved wrong,

but the worst is over and for one afternoon he doesn't
have to be the one keeping all those goddamned
kids from killing themselves in the back of the bus.

He's got a little time to wonder over these lie detectors,
that saw right through him, even joke about it
to Klein, who smiled a little, who really isn't a bad guy.

Here's Mitchell—a little wrong, a little shamed, no longer
a bus driver. But he's still here, still trying, still one of us.

Dad Hides His Shakiness by Telling a Story

Jerry Beiterman stops in every so often to see me.
The other day he took me out to the stockyards
east of town for lunch and a piece of pie. They're
famous for their pie, you know, they must make

twenty pies a morning. They've got a gal
all she does is make the pies. And they put
a huge piece on your plate, must be
a quarter pie, with ice cream. It's a meal

in itself. Old Jerry, he's a talker, always teasing
the women. They just laugh with him.
He says, "Oh, stop." They just laugh.
Old Jerry tells everybody in the restaurant

he had an operation on his rear end and the stitches
left quite a scar. Jerry went back to the doctor
and said, "I've got a vet who can sew up a cut
on my horse and never leave a scar and here

you've marked me for life!" (I sewed up his horse
once and it healed right over.) He's telling everybody
in the place. All the old farmers are laughing.
I said, "What are you doing, Jerry, showing everybody

your rear end?" Well, they all laughed at that.
They said, "That's right, Jerry, what do you need
to show off your rear end for?" You see, Jerry lived
through cancer himself. That's what he's talking about.

Caesura

This seems like someone else's house,
with people gathered in another room.
I'm frozen in a foyer, blinded, caught between

two worlds: the deathbed and the living room.
I sense a hand extended; I can't reach it.
I hear a voice—but does it speak to me?

I'm pinned in my experience, a knife-edged
loneliness. Damn them! They all seem
to live so easily. And if I join them,

won't the death room close behind me,
with its warmth, its quiet light, my father's breath
still resting in the lamplit air above the bed,

a blessing? The rage of Helen Keller,
child once sighted—now I understand. For once
I *had* a language. Once this was *my* house, my clear

and running sense of things. I want my healing
alphabet of water, want my voice, my words,
some meaning, to be again alive and still his daughter.

Dubrovnik

High over the city, on the rooftop terrace of my good hotel
I can hear the anthill of original city: no machinery
but the polyphonic hum of human voices. Below me,

the tiled roofs of Stari Grad, the city walls, the sea.
Ancient city of diplomats, protected from evil by the sea,
from disease by the fountain at the city gates, by watchtowers

and statesmanship, its progressive laws finally lost
to larger, more brutal systems. Once two cities, it's now
joined by the Stradun, its stone so polished by centuries

of feet that it shines as if covered in water, a brilliant
seam. I walk around the city walls, dizzy with height,
gripping the handrails, turning back at the highest point.

I am no bird. The air is a magnet sending current
through my spine: vertigo. I've traveled here alone,
grieving; to distract myself I read book after book

of local history: how the Turks impaled a common thief
by inserting a wooden stake, sharpened at one end,
six inches in diameter, into his anus, and pounding

with a wooden mallet, blow by deadening blow, expertly
guiding the stake through the wriggling body in order
not to kill the man too soon, around the heart,

until the stake emerged in the soft purpling place
between the collar bone and the neck; how the Croats, in a fit
of religious zeal, rounded up a village of Jews—men,

women and children—and set them one by one, terrified,
onto the conveyor belt of a slaughterhouse. Even the Nazis
were shocked. And what am I to understand—

that this world, seven islands planted in a brilliant ocean,
is peopled with entire nations of murderous fucks, but has no room
for one gentle man, who could not be saved, who continuously

cultivated the ground of kindness in himself and laid
his disappointments there to nourish something more beautiful?
I could step out into this nerved air, shimmering with sound,

and fall to the street. The crowd would gather, murmur, sweep
me into the sea, and disperse. The men who created horror
lived on, attended the birthday parties of grandchildren, drank

ordinary coffee. The world continues. A secret part of me
was relieved my father died before the worst of the world
could meet him in the street. What was he thinking—

bringing five new souls into the world with no protection
but kindness and the prayer he taught us, chanted every night:
deliver us from evil. Could he imagine me here, alone and murderous,

abandoned, sitting in the light reflected off human history,
off the ocean's brilliant shroud? This could be my burial
in air, poems pushing out of me like sharpened stakes.

Let the birds rip out my seams. Let me be a bird flying
straight out, far from the sight of shore. Let this city outlive me,
this city filled with ordinary people, who still drink coffee

every morning with the old ones still living in the house.

Stari Grad: Old City

Stradun: A main street running through the Old City, also called the Placa. It was originally
a water channel that separated two early settlements and was paved when the two
merged.

Nine

The first time a man talked to me that way
I was nine, perched on a piano bench
at Erlas' pool party, trying to balance
the paper plate of hotdog and potato salad
on my skinny legs and he
was a teenager, a retarded boy,
as thick and deep and hairy
as another creature altogether
and his mother was sitting right there
on a lounge chair and her drink
was in a glass with ice cubes
and he said, "How'd you like to come home with me,
    little girl?"
and I said, "No, thank you,"
and I watched and watched his mother
who didn't say anything
and maybe her hard eyes were saying
there is no rescue.

Words, Poems

Midnight, something is calling
me up through layers of sleep.
I'm carrying the ragged remnant

of dream: an old woman
watching kids swim in a pool.
They are words; they are poems.

Their skin is so thin it is blue
in places; life roars
in their ears. She watches the pulse

in their young chests as they shout
and wrestle and knows she could say
any thing, tell any story.

What was it she woke me to say?
Awake, now, remembering, I begin
to hear. The woods are still,

the cabin quiet—even the fridge
has stopped its striving. Only
the heater ticks and the dog

stirs. He stretches, recurls
and pushes his rump hard
against my side, as if comfort

were something we back into,
test, to see if it will hold
up. I realize nothing hurts,

none of my old injuries—
the broken spine shambling
and shifting, the torn hamstring,

the pious neck—even
my heart has stopped forcing
itself through the pinhole of grief.

This morning I woke in tears,
feeling my childless and loosening
body, with nothing to hold

but the loyal dog. Now
this stillness is a new space.
Something tells me this

is what home could feel like.
Something says, *These words
are alive in you. Hold them.*

Across the Tracks

Across the tracks, a man is thanking God.
He hangs easy in his yellow suit, his beard
lifts his face in praise.

> *Attention, passengers, an outbound train*
> *from the Loop will be arriving shortly*

and he raises his right hand freely to the sky and speaks to it:

> *Thank you. Thank you, Monica.*

Then he's quiet, leaning back against the handrail
with satisfaction, someone who has drunk deeply
from life and found it, found it.

Next announcement he adds a dance step,
a restrained and jubilant shuffle. It's a warm night.
Makes you feel sharp, you know, the sashay

of an open jacket, Monica on the P.A.,
this good concrete, this molting sky, this pigeon
swinging feathers, this stop called Western, this

arriving car, these sticky treads,
this side-to-side, this
good company on the train.

The Garden

The silver maple now reaches above my upstairs window.
This tree was once just a pole my parents planted, rising out

of baked clay. Forty years ago, I stood under it
and watched earthworms wither in my clumsy hands, in the air

reflected off overheated brick. Now the tree, gracious
brother to the house, has unfolded itself over a deck.

Below it, a crabapple, plum, mountain ash,
a little pond with a known frog that winters there.

Out in the yard, knobbed clay under a grass veneer,
but close to the house, a glossy blanket of myrtle and clematis.

I have brought my father home after several days in the hospital,
that seasonless hell. Now we can rest in this garden.

A woodpecker hammers on the house; goldfinches
and hummingbirds circle pots of flowers. The leaves move

and are moved by light and air—there is a spaciousness here.
I lean out of the window and feel the black dog

of fanged grief rising in me. It will split me open.
All this time they were growing this garden. Later, in the breeze

the maple makes for us, we eat dinner on the deck.
He cuts out the tenderest part of his steak

and places it on my plate, with a deft gesture of knife and fork.
"Try that, Terese," he says, "That's the tenderloin."

Allowing this to happen, my mother watches in a new silence.
Earlier I saw him turn to her and say, "See? We have

a *good* family." I accept his gift, taste the salt and blood,
the animal butter of it, think how he is still showing me

the good in things. Was it me, refusing to eat, all these years?
Was it me, making nothing out of something? Later, from my room,

I see them sitting on the deck in the evening light, his arm
around her shoulders. They are so small, sitting there.

He is telling her to keep the house. He is showing her
the garden they made, teaching her to see paradise.